Seas & Oceans

BOOK HOUSE
a SALARIYA *imprint*

Published in Great Britain in MMXIV by
Book House, an imprint of
The Salariya Book Company Ltd
25 Marlborough Place, Brighton BN1 1UB
www.salariya.com
www.book-house.co.uk

PB ISBN-13: 978-1-909645-77-6

SALARIYA

A CIP catalogue record for this book is available
from the British Library.

Printed and bound in China.

Visit our website at **www.book-house.co.uk**
or go to **www.salariya.com** for **free** electronic versions of:
You Wouldn't Want to be an Egyptian Mummy!
You Wouldn't Want to be a Roman Gladiator!
You Wouldn't Want to be a Polar Explorer!
You Wouldn't Want to sail on a 19th-Century Whaling Ship!

Visit
www.salariya.com
for our online catalogue and **free**
interactive web books.

PAPER FROM
SUSTAINABLE
FORESTS

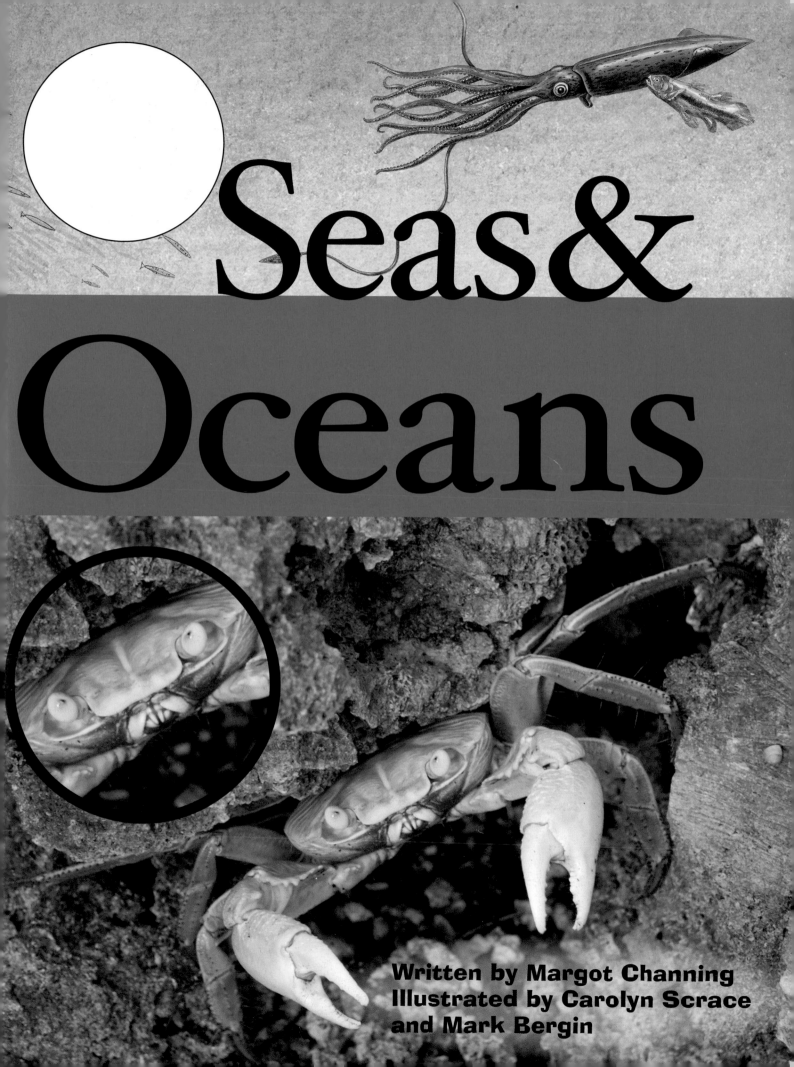

Seas & Oceans

Written by Margot Channing
Illustrated by Carolyn Scrace
and Mark Bergin

CONTENTS

WHAT ARE SEAS AND OCEANS?

Living on land, we easily forget that salty seawater covers most of the Earth. Four enormous hollows in the planet's surface hold the waters of the Arctic, Atlantic, Indian and Pacific oceans. The Pacific Ocean is the world's largest ocean. It is big enough to hold every continent on Earth and its deepest part could cover the highest mountain on land!

UNDERWATER MOUNTAIN

If the oceans were drained, the Earth's largest feature to be seen from space would be the mountain range that runs along the bottom of the oceans. It is more than 60,000 km long.

Mediterranean Sea

Seas and oceans hold 97 per cent of the world's water and cover almost 70 per cent of its surface. Large areas of partly enclosed ocean form the world's seas, such as the Mediterranean Sea.

Each layer of the sea is home to different forms of life. Only the sunlit surface is bright enough for plants to grow. Deep beneath the surface, there is very little light and it is very cold.

This book takes a closer look at the Earth's seas and oceans, from its shores, coral reefs and sunlit surfaces to its deepest, darkest, silent depths.

THE SEASHORE

The seashore, where the sea meets land, is full of life. Barnacles, limpets, sea anemones and seaweeds grip the rocky shores so tightly that even storm waves do not wrench them loose.

Herring gulls

Few creatures can hide on the shifting sandy surface of the shoreline. However, a few centimetres under the surface, many animals burrow for safety.

LOW TIDE

At low tide, shellfish close their shells to keep moisture inside so their bodies don't dry up. Shore fish are stranded in little pools, and crabs squeeze under shady rocks.

HIGH TIDE

At high tide, the flooded seashore comes to life. Creatures creep out of their hiding places to feed. Burrowing animals use tubes or feelers to suck in or grab tiny pieces of food carried in by the tide. Birds prey upon all these seashore creatures.

Sea anemones

Limpets

Seaweeds

Barnacles

CORAL REEFS

Coral reefs are rock-like formations that are found in the warm waters of tropical regions. A coral reef is made up of the skeletons of billions of tiny coral animals, called polyps. Each polyp attaches itself to the reef and builds up a hard, cup-shaped skeleton on the outside of its soft body. When a polyp dies, its skeleton remains, helping to build up the reef.

Coral

ALGAE AND POLYPS

Coral polyps are found only in warm, sunlit water where tiny plants called algae can grow inside the polyps' body. Algae release oxygen, which helps the polyps to breathe.

Coral grows in a variety of shapes. Some, like elkhorn, are branched. Others are rounded, like brain coral.

Blue surgeonfish

Sea turtle

Queen angelfish

WATER WORLD

The Great Barrier Reef, off the coast of Australia, is 1,930 km long. It is the longest coral reef in the world.

Sunlight that is strong enough for plants to grow only reaches the top 150 m of the sea. This is called the 'euphotic zone'. Tiny drifting plants float there alongside little animals that feed on them or on one another. Together, these plants and animals form a huge living organism called 'plankton'.

Ocean sunfish

CONTINENTAL SHELF

The continental shelf is found in the euphotic zone. It is the seabed that surrounds the Earth's continents. Many creatures live there, including eels and a huge variety of fish.

Sawfish

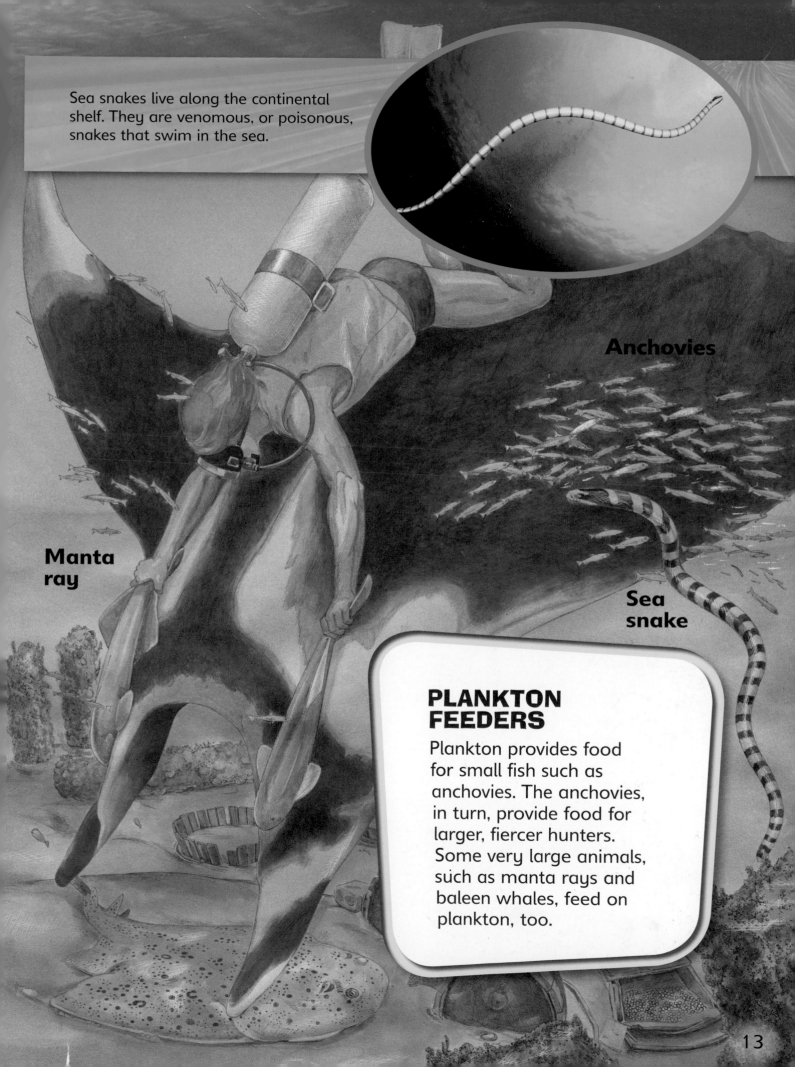

Sea snakes live along the continental shelf. They are venomous, or poisonous, snakes that swim in the sea.

Anchovies

Manta ray

Sea snake

PLANKTON FEEDERS

Plankton provides food for small fish such as anchovies. The anchovies, in turn, provide food for larger, fiercer hunters. Some very large animals, such as manta rays and baleen whales, feed on plankton, too.

THE MIDDLE OPEN SEA

Deep below the surface of the sea is the level known as middle open sea. This is also called the 'mesopelagic zone'. This level is between 150 and 1,000 m deep. It is too dark there for plants to grow. Creatures survive there by eating one another or any dead organisms that drift down from the ocean surface. Sometimes, they swim up towards the surface to feed on creatures that swim there.

Luminou prawn

Crustacean

MIDDLE SEA DEFENCE

Bonitos and other small fish swim in shoals for protection. Squid and jellyfish defend themselves with their deadly tentacles. Lantern fish have special chemicals that shine and sparkle like pearl buttons to help camouflage their shape.

Lantern fish

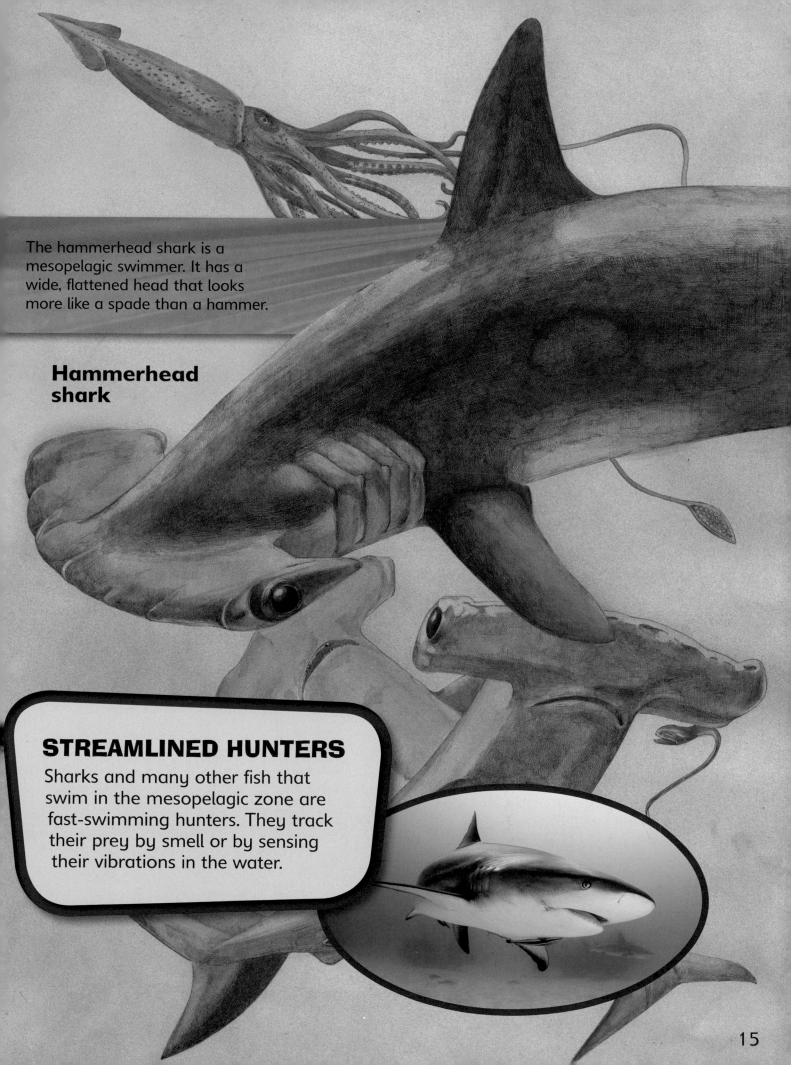

The hammerhead shark is a mesopelagic swimmer. It has a wide, flattened head that looks more like a spade than a hammer.

Hammerhead shark

STREAMLINED HUNTERS

Sharks and many other fish that swim in the mesopelagic zone are fast-swimming hunters. They track their prey by smell or by sensing their vibrations in the water.

THE DEEP OCEAN

The deep open ocean is also known as the 'bathypelagic zone'. This pitch black layer is found 1,000 – 3,000 m below the ocean surface. At this depth, food is hard to find, so fewer creatures swim there than in the mesopelagic layer above.

FLABBY FISH

Most of the fish that swim in the bathypelagic layer have weak, flabby bodies. They ambush passing prey, rather than chasing it through the sea. The deep-sea anglerfish attracts its prey with a light that glows at the end of a 'fishing rod' on top of its head.

Giant squid

Oarfish

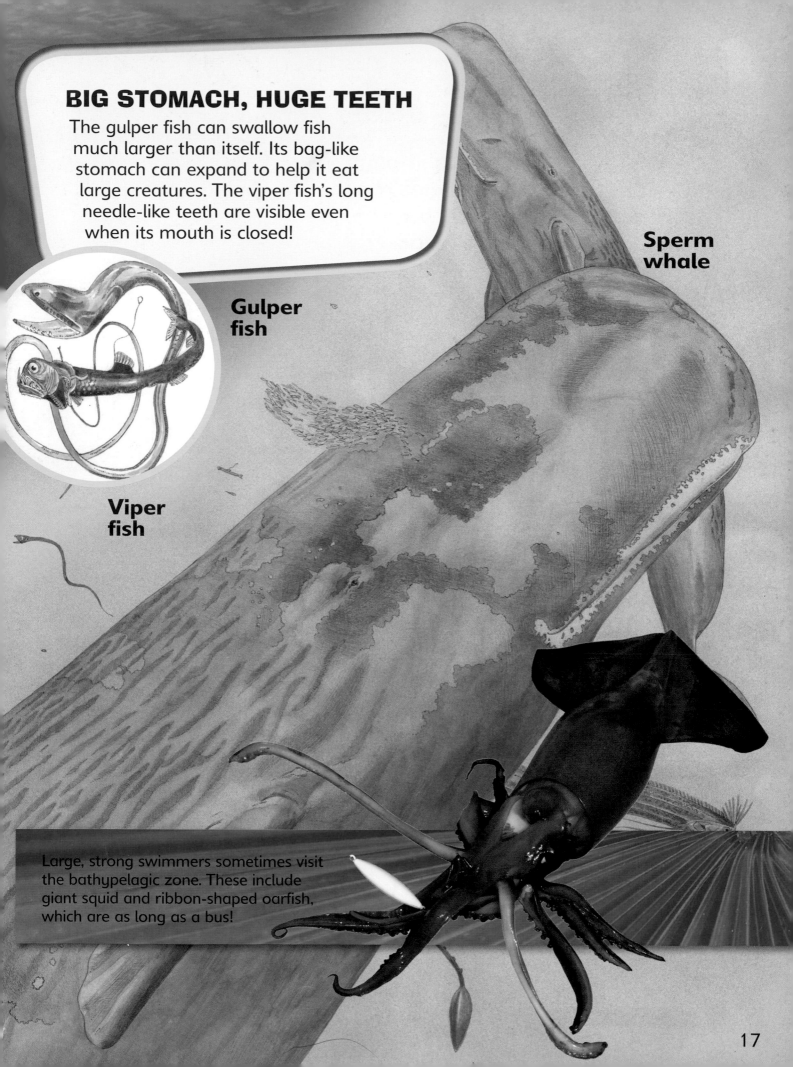

BIG STOMACH, HUGE TEETH

The gulper fish can swallow fish much larger than itself. Its bag-like stomach can expand to help it eat large creatures. The viper fish's long needle-like teeth are visible even when its mouth is closed!

Gulper fish

Viper fish

Sperm whale

Large, strong swimmers sometimes visit the bathypelagic zone. These include giant squid and ribbon-shaped oarfish, which are as long as a bus!

THE DEEP

Strange-looking fish and other creatures swim or crawl around the deepest level of the ocean. This layer, called the 'abyssal zone', is 3,000 – 11,000 m below the ocean surface. The water pressure at this depth is huge and the temperature is almost freezing.

FINDING FOOD

Creatures of the abyssal zone eat dead plants and animals that sink down from the higher layers of water above.

Deep-sea anglerfish

BOTTOM LIVING

The most common creature in the abyssal zone is the rat tail. This fish has a long end to its tail, rather like a rat's tail.

Rat tail

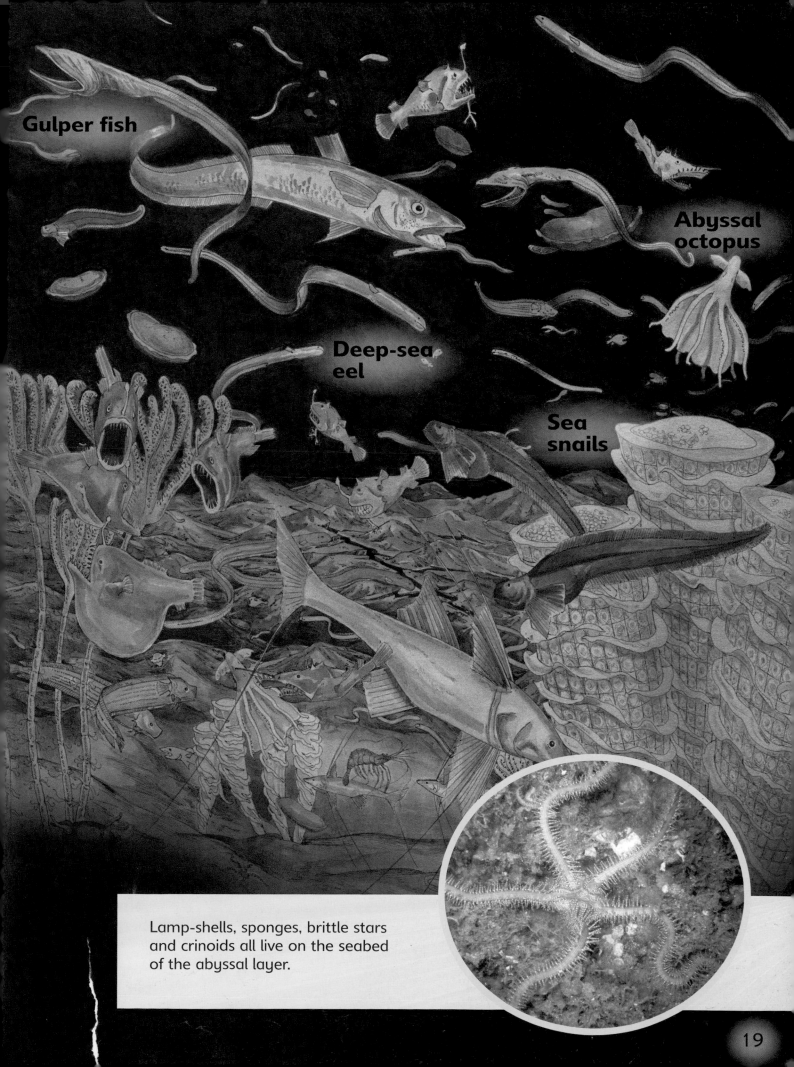

Gulper fish

Abyssal octopus

Deep-sea eel

Sea snails

Lamp-shells, sponges, brittle stars and crinoids all live on the seabed of the abyssal layer.

TSUNAMIS

*T*su is Japanese for 'overflowing', *nami* means 'wave'. A tsunami is a giant ocean wave that overflows the land. Tsunamis are created by sudden movements of the seabed that are caused by earthquakes or volcanic eruptions.

CREATING A TSUNAMI

An underwater earthquake or a volcanic eruption can suddenly force the seabed to shift dramatically up or down. This disturbs the layers of water above the seabed. Huge ripples of water expand outwards in all directions across the ocean. These are tsunamis.

Tsunami

HITTING THE SHORE

As a tsunami nears the shore, the waves get higher. Tsunamis have been known to rise to 18 m on flat, low-lying shores and to more than 30 m at the head of V-shaped inlets.

Tsunamis sweep inshore, smashing buildings, uprooting trees and tossing vehicles around like tiny toys.

21

OIL AND GAS RIGS

Artificial islands peep above the water in parts of the North Sea, Arctic Ocean, Gulf of Mexico and other offshore waters. These islands are the tops of oil and gas rigs that rise from the seabed.

TRANSPORTING A RIG

The steel or concrete towers of most rigs are built on land. They are then towed out to sea by tugs and erected on the ocean floor. Many rigs stand in shallow water, but some are in water that is more than 200 m deep.

FIXING A RIG

Rigs are fixed to the seabed by platforms. A tension leg platform is a floating platform held to the seabed by jointed legs. A steel jacket platform rests on a steel frame that is pinned to the seabed. The gravity platform sits on concrete legs that are anchored to the seabed by their great weight.

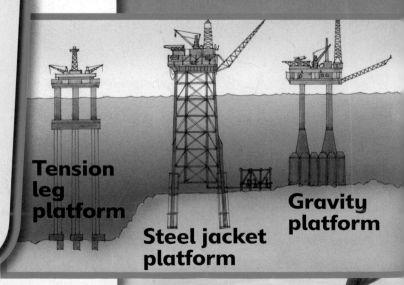

Tension leg platform

Steel jacket platform

Gravity platform

Workers and supplies are transported to and from a rig by boat or by helicopter. There are special helicopter landing pads on rigs.

Oil rig

DEEP-SEA FISHING

A modern fishing ship uses an underwater 'seeing eye' called a sonar. This device shows an image of the surrounding ocean. Sonars send out sound pulses. The echo from a sound pulse changes if it encounters a shoal of fish. The signals on the ship's radar alert the captain to exactly where to fish.

FISHING NETS

A trawl net is designed to catch fish at the bottom of the sea. A purse seine is drawn around a shoal of fish near the surface. It is closed with a cable so the fish cannot escape. A beam trawl is a large net held open by a wood or metal beam.

Freezer

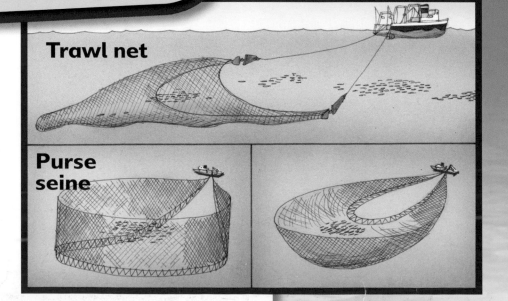

Trawl net

Purse seine

DANGEROUS FISHING

Deep-sea fishing used to be very dangerous. Small boats could easily be sunk in a storm. Today, radioed weather forecasts warn fishermen of storms.

Storm

When a catch of fish is pulled onboard, it is stored in freezers in the ship's hold. This keeps the fish fresh until it can be picked up by a smaller fishing boat and taken to shore.

SUBMARINES

Submarines are ships that can travel both on the sea and deep beneath its surface. When a submarine is ready to submerge, it must be made watertight. The ballast tanks are then filled with seawater until the submarine is so heavy that it sinks.

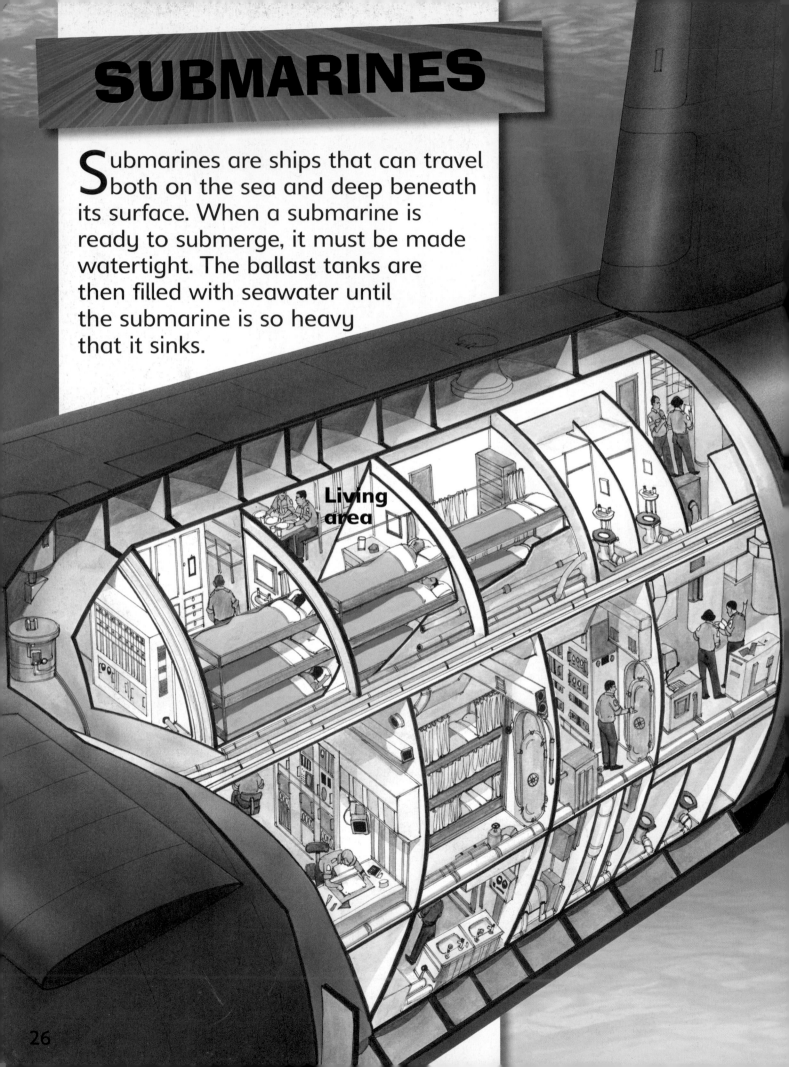

Living area

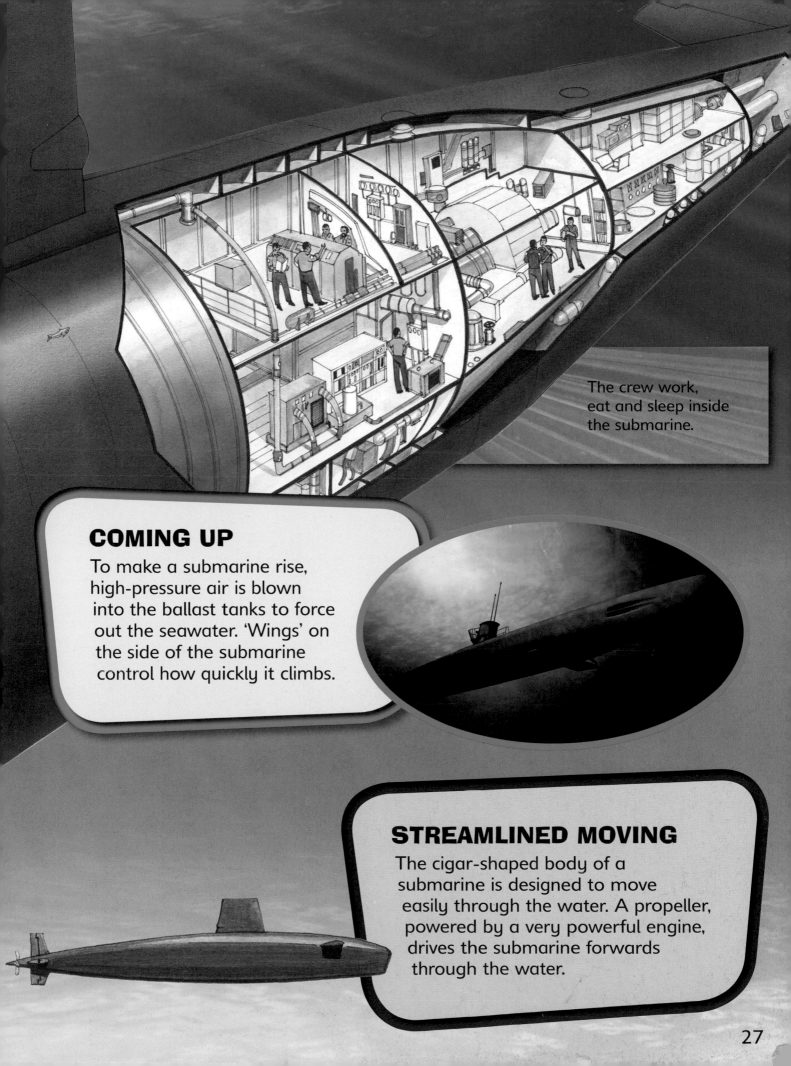

The crew work, eat and sleep inside the submarine.

COMING UP

To make a submarine rise, high-pressure air is blown into the ballast tanks to force out the seawater. 'Wings' on the side of the submarine control how quickly it climbs.

STREAMLINED MOVING

The cigar-shaped body of a submarine is designed to move easily through the water. A propeller, powered by a very powerful engine, drives the submarine forwards through the water.

EXPLORING THE OCEANS

Oceans cover 70 per cent of the Earth's surface, yet, until 1960, no human had ever seen the seabed. Since then, we have made remarkable discoveries about the oceans, from deep-sea vents that shoot out boiling water, to the astonishing deep-sea creatures that live there. Who knows how many more mysteries we have yet to discover?

EARTH'S DEEPEST TRENCH

In 1960, two men named Jacques Piccard and Donald Walsh travelled nearly 11 km below the ocean surface. In a vessel named the *Trieste*, the pair journeyed to the bottom of the Marianas Trench, the deepest trench in the world.

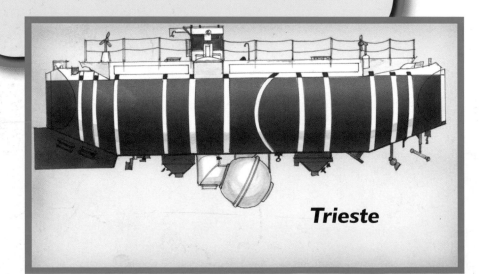

Trieste

Jason Junior

SUBMERSIBLE DIVING

Alvin is a research vessel that is used to discover more about the oceans. *Alvin* has a 'robot' called *Jason Junior*, which is used to travel into places that are too small for *Alvin* to reach.

In 1985, *Alvin* provided the world's first look at the *Titanic* since its sinking in 1912.

TITANIC

GLOSSARY

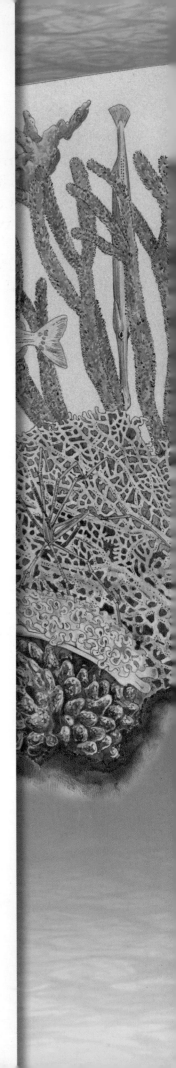

Abyssal zone the pitch-black bottom layer of the ocean, from 3,000 to 11,000 m deep.

Algae simple plants made of one cell or chains of cells. Algae live in moist places and include seaweeds.

Baleen whales toothless whales with a fringe of baleen (rows of bristles) that hangs down from the upper jaw. The baleen traps small creatures as the whale swims along with its mouth open.

Bathypelagic zone the dark ocean layer, between 1,000 and 3,000 m deep.

Brittle stars spindly-armed relatives of the starfish.

Continental shelf the shallow underwater rim of the continents, averaging about 200 m deep.

Coral reefs rock-like formations made of the skeletons of billions of tiny sea creatures called coral polyps.

Euphotic zone the uppermost, sunlit layer of the ocean where seaweeds and other plants can grow, up to 150 m deep.

Gulper fish thin, deep-sea fish with an enormous mouth and a bag-like stomach.

Mesopelagic layer the middle open sea, from 150 to 1,000 m deep.

Ray a type of fish with a wide, flat shape. Its skeleton is not bony but gristly like a shark's.

Shark fierce, streamlined fish with a gristly skeleton. Sharks eat other fish and some mammals, such as seals. A few species of large shark sometimes attack human swimmers.

Squid ten-armed sea creatures that are related to octopuses. A squid seizes its prey with its tentacles and then kills it with a bite. A squid quickly propels itself through the water by forcing jets of water out of its body through a narrow tube.

Viper fish a deep-sea fish with huge fangs that look similar to the fangs of a type of snake called a viper.

INDEX